Weekly
Real-World
Writing

GRADES 1–2

Writing: Guadalupe Lopez
Content Editing: Kathleen Jorgensen
Lisa Vitarisi Mathews
Copy Editing: Cathy Harber
Art Direction: Yuki Meyer
Illustration: Mary Rojas
Cover Design: Yuki Meyer
Design/Production: Paula Acojido
Yuki Meyer

EMC 6077

Visit
teaching-standards.com
to view a correlation
of this book.
This is a free service.

**Correlated to
Current Standards**

**Congratulations on your purchase of some of the
finest teaching materials in the world.**

*Photocopying the pages in this book
is permitted for <u>single-classroom use only</u>.
Making photocopies for additional classes
or schools is prohibited.*

For information about other Evan-Moor products, call 1-800-777-4362,
fax 1-800-777-4332, or visit our website, www.evan-moor.com.
Entire contents © 2021 EVAN-MOOR CORP.
18 Lower Ragsdale Drive, Monterey, CA 93940-5746. Printed in USA.

CPSIA: McNaughton & Gunn, Saline, MI USA [2/2022]

CONTENTS

What's in *Weekly Real-World Writing*

Most writing programs cover the essentials of academic writing that students need to succeed in school: grammar and mechanics, structure of sentences and paragraphs, and the essential parts of fiction and nonfiction genres. While some academic writing may play a role in students' everyday lives, we use many other types of writing on a daily basis—on paper, online, and in graphic form. This series covers many of those writing formats.

24 Engaging Units

Real-world writing happens when there is a reason to write. The format of the writing often follows the writing purpose. This book focuses on six common writing purposes: self-expression, information, evaluation, inquiry, analysis, and persuasion. Within each purpose are four units, each featuring a different writing format. The first two units in each purpose section have been developed for students who are beginning writers; the second two are intended for students who have some writing experience.

Unit Features

Units are designed to fit into a weekly lesson plan. Each 5-page unit provides a page of information for the teacher, followed by modeling for the students, a graphic organizer, and writing tasks.

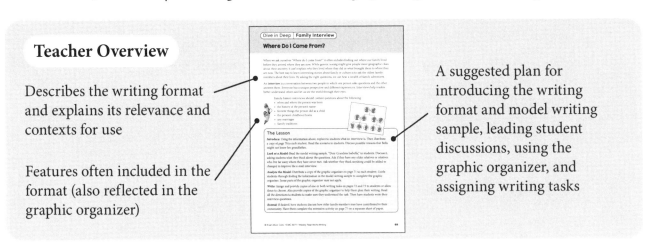

Teacher Overview

Describes the writing format and explains its relevance and contexts for use

Features often included in the format (also reflected in the graphic organizer)

A suggested plan for introducing the writing format and model writing sample, leading student discussions, using the graphic organizer, and assigning writing tasks

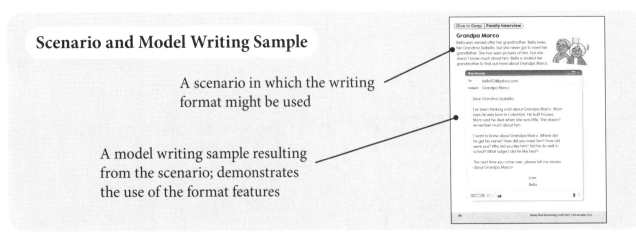

Scenario and Model Writing Sample

A scenario in which the writing format might be used

A model writing sample resulting from the scenario; demonstrates the use of the format features

Format-Specific Graphic Organizer

A way to collect notes for the format in the unit; includes sections for most of the format features listed in the Teacher Overview

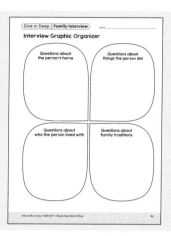

Writing Tasks

Two opportunities to practice writing in the given format, along with response space

An extension activity that provides an opportunity for students to relate the format to their own lives

Student Rubrics

Two student rubrics are provided, one for formal writing and one for informal writing. These are general, non-format-specific rubrics to remind students of the general aspects of effective writing. (pages 7 and 8)

Have students use the formal writing rubric to check formal formats, such as a product review or a presentation. Have them use the informal writing rubric to check informal formats, such as a journal entry or a choice list.

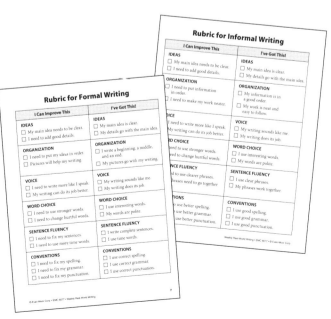

Ways to Use *Weekly Real-World Writing*

Connections for Your Students

You can use the units in this series in many ways. Use the units to extend your primary writing program, providing additional writing opportunities. Use them to augment learning in other content areas. For example, you can use the Set of Rules unit to have students process their thoughts on citizenship, community, and laws that you are studying in social studies. You can use the Weather unit to help students differentiate descriptions of weather from their opinions about it in science. You can use the Thank-you Note unit to thank a guest speaker who has visited your class. Be on the lookout for everyday opportunities to relate units to your students' real lives.

The Importance of Discussion

Discussing the scenario and the model writing sample does more than show students why people write. Just as important as what the writer wants to say is making sure the audience understands what the writer intended. The writer must understand the audience's perspective: Does the audience merely lack knowledge? Are they curious about something? Do they have an attitude or belief that is different from the writer's? Will they most likely be happy, sad, or defensive about the writer's message? By anticipating the audience's perspective, the writer can choose words carefully and organize the writing to avoid an unwanted reaction. Discussing both the writer's and the reader's perspectives in the unit scenario will help students understand how writing, feelings, and relationships are related.

Use of Graphic Organizers

The main purpose of the graphic organizer is to help students get started and plan what they will write. However, it can also be used to analyze the model writing sample. Lead students to connect a sample format's components with the graphic organizer by asking questions such as, "Directions show order. What text in the sample tells what you do second? Write it in the 'Step 2' box on your graphic organizer," or "You make a greeting card for a reason. Why is Selena making a card in the sample? Write it in the 'Why am I giving it?' section on your graphic organizer."

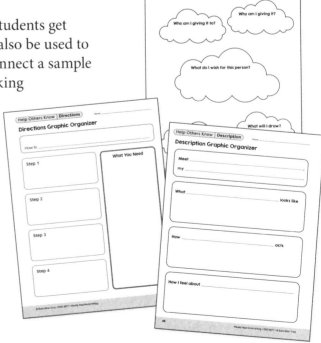

Weekly Real-World Writing • EMC 6077 • © Evan-Moor Corp.

Rubric for Formal Writing

I Can Improve This	I've Got This!
IDEAS ☐ My main idea needs to be clear. ☐ I need to add good details.	**IDEAS** ☐ My main idea is clear. ☐ My details go with the main idea.
ORGANIZATION ☐ I need to put my ideas in order. ☐ Pictures will help my writing.	**ORGANIZATION** ☐ I write a beginning, a middle, and an end. ☐ My pictures go with my writing.
VOICE ☐ I need to write more like I speak. ☐ My writing can do its job better.	**VOICE** ☐ My writing sounds like me. ☐ My writing does its job.
WORD CHOICE ☐ I need to use stronger words. ☐ I need to change hurtful words.	**WORD CHOICE** ☐ I use interesting words. ☐ My words are polite.
SENTENCE FLUENCY ☐ I need to fix my sentences. ☐ I need to use more time words.	**SENTENCE FLUENCY** ☐ I write complete sentences. ☐ I use time words.
CONVENTIONS ☐ I need to fix my spelling. ☐ I need to fix my grammar. ☐ I need to fix my punctuation.	**CONVENTIONS** ☐ I use correct spelling. ☐ I use correct grammar. ☐ I use correct punctuation.

Rubric for Informal Writing

I Can Improve This	I've Got This!
IDEAS ☐ My main idea needs to be clear. ☐ I need to add good details.	**IDEAS** ☐ My main idea is clear. ☐ My details go with the main idea.
ORGANIZATION ☐ I need to put information in order. ☐ I need to make my work neater.	**ORGANIZATION** ☐ My information is in a good order. ☐ My work is neat and easy to follow.
VOICE ☐ I need to write more like I speak. ☐ My writing can do its job better.	**VOICE** ☐ My writing sounds like me. ☐ My writing does its job.
WORD CHOICE ☐ I need to use stronger words. ☐ I need to change hurtful words.	**WORD CHOICE** ☐ I use interesting words. ☐ My words are polite.
SENTENCE FLUENCY ☐ I need to use clearer phrases. ☐ My phrases need to go together better.	**SENTENCE FLUENCY** ☐ I use clear phrases. ☐ My phrases work together.
CONVENTIONS ☐ I need to use better spelling. ☐ I need to use better grammar. ☐ I need to use better punctuation.	**CONVENTIONS** ☐ I use good spelling. ☐ I use good grammar. ☐ I use good punctuation.

 Weekly Real-World Writing • EMC 6077 • © Evan-Moor Corp.

Please Write Back

Friends and family enjoy hearing about our lives. A friendly letter is a good way to share personal updates. What's new? How's it going? People look forward to reading family update letters that arrive in holiday cards. It's a great way to catch up with those who don't live close by.

But why write letters when online communication is so fast and convenient? We can share information through e-mail, texts, or social media. Writing a letter, in our own handwriting and on our choice of stationery, adds a personal touch to our communication. It gives the recipient something tangible to hold onto.

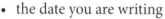

A friendly letter should contain the following:

- the date you are writing
- a greeting to the recipient
- news about what you have been doing or feeling
- questions about what the recipient has been doing or feeling
- a closing and your name
- illustrations, photos, or emojis as desired

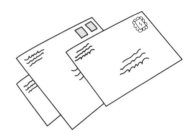

The Lesson

Introduce: Using the information above, explain to students what a friendly letter is. Then distribute a copy of page 10 to each student. Read the scenario to students. Discuss it, asking students if a friend has ever moved away. Ask if any relatives live far away.

Look at a Model: Read the model writing sample, "Dear Grandma," to students. Talk about the information Dulce shares. Ask them how Dulce's grandmother might feel as she reads the letter. Ask whether they think anything could be added or changed in the letter.

Analyze the Model: Distribute a copy of the graphic organizer on page 11 to each student. Guide students through finding the information in the model writing sample to complete the graphic organizer. Some parts of the graphic organizer may not apply.

Write: Assign and provide copies of one or both writing tasks on pages 12 and 13 to students or allow them to choose. Also distribute a copy of the graphic organizer to help them plan their writing. Read all the directions to students to make sure they understand the task. Then have students write their friendly messages.

Extend: If desired, have students brainstorm examples of people in their own lives who would like to receive a friendly letter from them. Have them complete the extension activity on page 13 on a separate sheet of paper.

Grandma Moved Away

Dulce's grandmother used to live next door. Now she lives in another city far away. Dulce misses her grandma. Dulce wrote to her grandma to tell her about school.

September 20, 2021

Dear Grandma,

How are you? I'm doing fine. I started first grade! I have a new friend. His name is Leo. My teacher is Miss Sanders.

I miss you, Grandma. I hope you visit soon. We can go to the Butterfly Garden. Please write back.

Love,
Dulce

Friendly Letter Graphic Organizer

_____
Date

Dear _____,
Greeting

News and Questions

_____,
Closing

_____
Your name

All About Me Writing Task #1

Pretend that it is summer. You will have a new teacher in the fall.
His name is Mr. Ato. He wrote a letter to welcome you.
Write back to Mr. Ato. Tell him about yourself.

I Miss You Writing Task #2

Pretend that your friend moved away. Write a letter to tell him or her what is new with you.

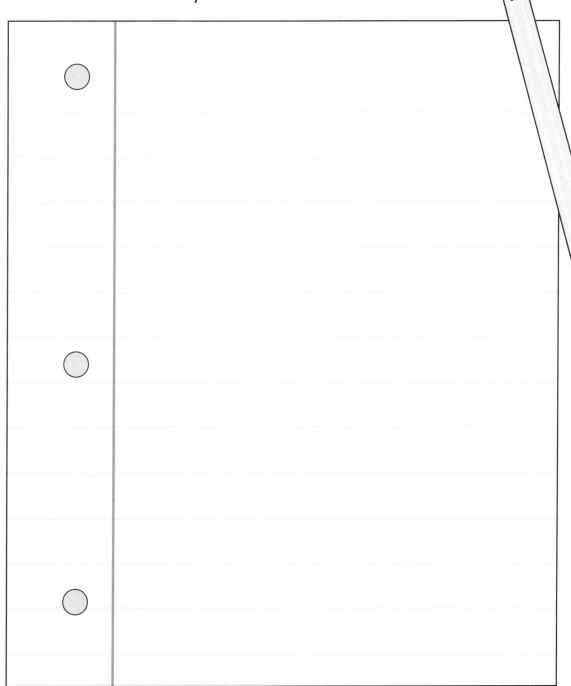

Extension Activity

Think of someone you miss. Write a letter to that person.

I Appreciate You

Writing thank-you notes is a simple and thoughtful way of showing appreciation. Adults send them to acknowledge wedding gifts or to thank someone for a job interview, but there are many occasions in which children can write thank-you notes. They can write them after receiving gifts for their birthday or other special days. They can thank a teacher, a babysitter, or a librarian who helped them. A child who has had a broken arm, his or her tonsils removed, or any medical condition might want to write a thank-you note for the care received.

Writing a handwritten note takes time; that's how the gift giver knows that he or she is truly appreciated. The note should be sent in a timely manner.

A thank-you note should contain the following:

- a greeting to the recipient
- a mention of *what* is being appreciated
- an explanation of *why* it is appreciated
- a closing and your name
- a positive feel
- illustrations, photos, or emojis as desired

The Lesson

Introduce: Using the information above, explain to students what a thank-you note is. Then distribute a copy of page 15 to each student. Read the scenario to students. Discuss it, asking students about gifts they have given. Ask how they go about choosing the perfect gift and how they hope the recipient will feel. Ask how they feel when someone says "thank you."

Look at a Model: Read the model writing sample, "Dear Paco," to students. Talk about the gift that Paco chose for his teacher. Ask them how Paco probably felt when he received a thank-you note from his teacher.

Analyze the Model: Distribute a copy of the graphic organizer on page 16 to each student. Guide students through finding the information in the model writing sample to complete the graphic organizer. Some parts of the graphic organizer may not apply.

Write: Assign and provide copies of one or both writing tasks on pages 17 and 18 to students or allow them to choose. Also provide copies of the graphic organizer to help them plan their writing. Read all the directions to students to make sure they understand the task. Then have students write their thank-you notes.

Extend: If desired, have students brainstorm situations in their own lives in which they received a gift or appreciated something that someone did. Have them complete the extension activity on page 18 on a separate sheet of paper.

A Nice Gift

Paco knows that his teacher, Ms. Pike, loves plants. Paco gave Ms. Pike a spider plant at the end of the school year. Ms. Pike wrote a note to thank Paco.

Dear Paco,

Thank you for the pretty spider plant! You know how much I love plants. I have the perfect spot for it at home. I will hang it in my kitchen.

I liked having you in class this year. Have fun in second grade!

Your teacher,

Ms. Pike

Thank-you Note Graphic Organizer

Who are you thanking?

What did the person do?

Why do you like it?

How can you end the note?

Dear Teacher Writing Task #1

Pretend that it is the end of the school year.
How did your teacher help you?
Write him or her a thank-you note.

A Great Gift Writing Task #2

Pretend that your uncle gave you a red bike. It is your
first bike! Write a note to thank your uncle.

 Extension Activity

Think of someone who did something nice for you.
Write a thank-you note to that person.

Thinking of You

Happy birthday! Get well soon! Good job! I miss you! Students may be most familiar with birthday and holiday cards. There are many other occasions in life that call for expressions of love, kindness, sorrow, and joy. Cards can congratulate someone for an accomplishment or encourage someone to keep trying. They can wish someone well before surgery, starting at a new school, going away to camp, or starting a new job. They can help someone apologize, mourn a loss, or laugh at something silly.

Ready-made greeting cards can be bought almost anywhere, but a handmade card is one of a kind. Whether you make, give, or receive a card, it creates joy for everyone concerned. A thoughtful card is a gift in itself.

A greeting card should contain the following:

- images and words on the front of the card
- a message on the inside of the card
- the names of the recipient and sender
- artwork that reflects the type of card
- language that conveys the appropriate emotion

The Lesson

Introduce: Using the information above, explain to students what a greeting card is. Show them a variety of store-bought cards. Note the format of the cards. Then distribute a copy of page 20 to each student. Read the scenario to students. Discuss it, asking students about greeting cards they have seen in the store. Ask how they go about choosing the perfect card.

Look at a Model: Read the model writing sample, "Get Well Soon!" to students. Talk about the feeling that Selena is expressing. Ask students how they think Jake felt when he got the card from his friend.

Analyze the Model: Distribute a copy of the graphic organizer on page 21 to each student. Guide students through finding the information in the model writing sample to complete the graphic organizer. Some parts of the graphic organizer may not apply.

Write: Assign and provide copies of one or both writing tasks on pages 22 and 23 to students or allow them to choose. Also provide copies of the graphic organizer to help them plan their writing. Read all the directions to students to make sure they understand the task. Then have students make their cards.

Extend: If desired, have students brainstorm situations in their own lives in which they received a greeting card or sent one. Have them complete the extension activity on page 23 on a separate sheet of paper.

Jake's Fall

Selena has a friend named Jake. Jake fell off his skateboard. He broke his leg! He needs to stay home. Selena made Jake a card to help him feel better.

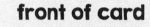
front of card

get-well wish

Get Well Soon!

Dear Jake,

   I'm sad that you broke your leg. I hope you feel better soon. We miss you at school.

   Your friend,

   Selena

Greeting Card Graphic Organizer

Who am I giving it to?

Why am I giving it?

What do I wish for this person?

How do I feel?

What will I draw?

Happy Birthday Writing Task #1

Pretend that it is your friend's birthday. Make a card for your friend.
Draw art on the card.

front of card

birthday greeting

I'm Sorry Writing Task #2

Pretend that you were mean to your friend. Your friend is sad. You are sorry. You hope you are still friends. Make your friend a card. Draw on the front.

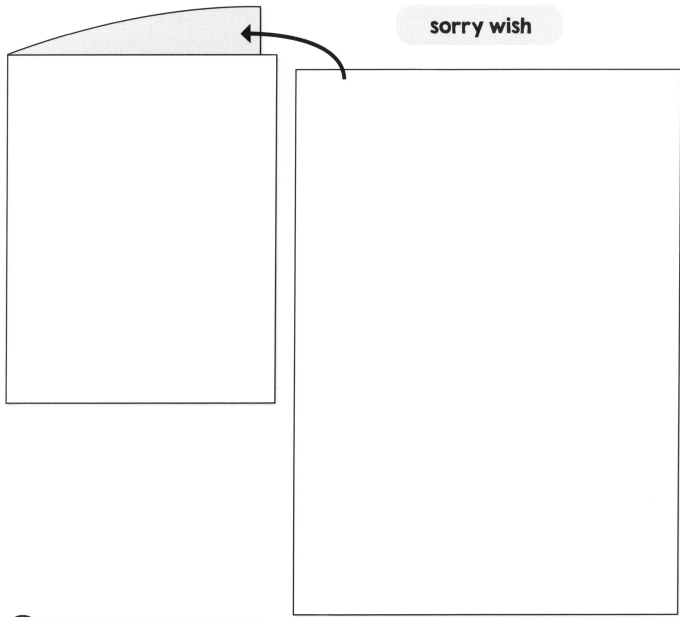

front of card

sorry wish

😎 Extension Activity

Think of someone you love. Make a special card for that person.

Remembering the Day

Keeping a journal or a diary helps us record details of events in our daily lives and our feelings and opinions about those events. Journal writing is fun when done regularly and freely, without the pressure of a writing assignment. Some people add doodles or drawings to their narratives. Journal entries may be recorded in a spiral-bound notebook, in a store-bought journal, in a journal made of sheets of paper stapled together, or on a computer.

Journals have entries; each time you write, that's an **entry**. Writing about what happened each day and how it felt helps students process and make sense of events. It lets them think about their actions and reactions as well as their developing relationships with friends and adults.

A journal entry should contain the following:
- the date
- details of what happened during the day
- feelings about what happened
- drawings as needed

My Journal

The Lesson

Introduce: Using the information above, explain to students what a journal or a diary is. Then distribute a copy of page 25 to each student. Read the scenario to students. Discuss it, asking students about trips they have taken. Ask how they can remember details of their trips.

Look at a Model: Read the model writing sample, "My Trip," to students. Talk about the details that Henry is recording. Why did he write about his cousin? What was special about the second day? How did Henry feel about what he did on those days?

Analyze the Model: Distribute a copy of the graphic organizer on page 26 to each student. Guide students through finding the information in the model writing sample to complete the graphic organizer. Some parts of the graphic organizer may not apply.

Write: Assign and provide copies of one or both writing tasks on pages 27 and 28 to students or allow them to choose. Also provide copies of the graphic organizer to help them plan their writing. Read all the directions to students to make sure they understand the task. Then have students write their journal entries.

Extend: If desired, have students talk about recent events in their lives. Have them complete the extension activity on page 28 on a separate sheet of paper.

Chicago Fun

Henry and his family are in Chicago. They are visiting
Uncle Marco and Henry's cousins. They see things in
the city. Henry writes about the trip in his journal.

My Trip

June 20

I met my cousin Ariana.
She is 12 years old. She
has a turtle named
Shelly. Ariana is funny.
She makes Shelly talk.

Hi. I'm Shelly!

June 21

Today we went to Navy
Pier. We rode the big
Ferris wheel. It went
very high, but I wasn't
scared. It was a sunny
day. The lake was blue
and calm. Later, we ate
pizza. It was so good!

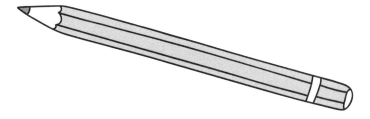

Journal Entry Graphic Organizer

What happened?

Who was there?

Where did it happen?

How did I feel?

What will I draw?

Weekly Real-World Writing • EMC 6077 • © Evan-Moor Corp.

Name _____

My Weekend Writing Task #1

How was your weekend? What did you do? Who were you with?
Draw a picture. Write about it.

Date: _____

My Day Writing Task #2

What kind of a day is today? Color the emoji that matches how you feel.
Write about it.

Date: _____

How I feel:

This is why:

😎 **Extension Activity**

Make your own journal. Fold 7 sheets of paper. Have a grown-up
make two holes where it folds. Put string through the holes.
Tie the string. Now you can write!

Let's Celebrate!

Writing an invitation is a polite way to ask someone to come to an event. You might invite friends to a party or a movie. You could invite family to a wedding or a school graduation. A handwritten invitation may be decorated to make the event look fun and appealing. The decoration might look like the event. For example, an invitation to a skating party might show a pair of skates. A beach party might show a sandcastle or a beach ball.

Invitations also provide necessary information about the event. Without this information, the invited guests wouldn't know where to go, when to arrive, or what to bring. The event might require a gift, food, an activity cost, or some other contribution. The invitation also tells guests how to respond to say whether they are attending. That allows the host of the event to plan better.

An invitation should contain the following:
- the date and time
- the location and address
- the purpose of the event
- what the guests should bring
- how to respond to the event host
- graphics that relate to the event

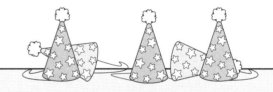

The Lesson

Introduce: Using the information above, explain to students what an invitation is. Then distribute a copy of page 30 to each student. Read the scenario to students. Discuss it, asking students if they have ever gone to a birthday or holiday party or to a special celebration. Make a list of familiar events that people send invitations for.

Look at a Model: Read the model writing sample, "Kari's Chalk Party," to students. Point out the kinds of information given. Ask them why each one is important. Ask whether they think anything could be added or changed in the invitation.

Analyze the Model: Distribute a copy of the graphic organizer on page 31 to each student. Guide students through finding the information in the model writing sample to complete the graphic organizer. Some parts of the graphic organizer may not apply.

Write: Assign and provide copies of one or both writing tasks on pages 32 and 33 to students or allow them to choose. Also provide copies of the graphic organizer to help them plan their writing. Read all the directions to students to make sure they understand the task. Then have students write and decorate their invitations.

Extend: If desired, have students brainstorm situations in their own lives in which writing an invitation would be appropriate. Have them complete the extension activity on page 33 on a separate sheet of paper.

A Chalk Party!

Kari likes art. She also likes to play outside. She will have a party with colored chalk. Her friends will come over. Everyone will draw colorful pictures on the sidewalk! Then they will eat ice cream.

Kari made an invitation for each friend. It tells all about the chalk party.

Please come to
Kari's Chalk Party

We will draw art on the sidewalk.

We have lots of chalk.
Later, we will eat ice cream!

It is on May 15 at 1:00.

It is at Kari's house, 25 Pine Street.

We want to make chalk art.

Bring one dollar.

Call 555-1616 to say Yes 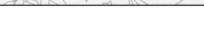 or No 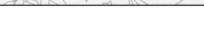.

Please come! It will be fun!

Name _____

Invitation Graphic Organizer

Invitation

When is it? _____

Where is it? _____

What is it for? _____

What should guests bring? _____

How should they tell you if they can come?

_____

What else do you want to tell them?

_____

How should you decorate the invitations?

_____

Graduation Party Writing Task #1

Pretend that your younger brother or sister is graduating from kindergarten. Your family is having a party to celebrate. Write an invitation.

Holiday Party Writing Task #2

Pretend that you are having a Valentine's Day party. Write an invitation.

😎 Extension Activity

Think of a special day that you want friends to come over and celebrate.
Write an invitation to invite them.

Follow the Rules

Everyone needs to follow rules, including grown-ups and children. We follow rules at home, at school, at play, and at work. Every home or classroom has its own set of rules that meets its needs. For example, you can run on a playground but not in a store. You can laugh in a store but not in a library. There are different rules where people play, work, or travel. Rules might be different when you are inside or outside. A rule that a whole community must follow is called a **law**.

We need rules to set expectations, promote fairness, and keep everyone safe. Without rules, someone might never get a turn at a game. Classrooms would be disorderly. At home, chores would never get done. Rules are usually posted where everyone in the group can see them.

A set of rules should contain the following:
- a title indicating whom the rules are for
- a list with bulleted or numbered items
- expectations for behavior
- imperative sentences with simple wording
- a positive tone

The Lesson

Introduce: Using the information above, explain to students what a set of rules is. Then distribute a copy of page 35 to each student. Read the scenario to students. Discuss it, asking students about different places that have rules. Ask how breaking a rule can make other people feel.

Look at a Model: Read the model writing sample, "Classroom Rules," to students. Talk about the different sections. Is there another way to group the rules? Ask students to choose a rule and explain why a class should follow it.

Analyze the Model: Distribute a copy of the graphic organizer on page 36 to each student. Guide students through finding the information in the model writing sample to complete the graphic organizer. Some parts of the graphic organizer may not apply.

Write: Assign copies of one or both writing tasks on pages 37 and 38 to students or allow them to choose. Also provide copies of the graphic organizer to help them plan their writing. Read all the directions to students to make sure they understand the task. Then have students write their sets of rules.

Extend: If desired, have students brainstorm a setting in which people are expected to follow rules. Have them complete the extension activity on page 38 on a separate sheet of paper.

First Day of School

On the first day of school, Miss Ellen and her class made a list of class rules. She asked students, "What should happen in the classroom?" She wrote what they said. Then she made a poster. She put it on the wall.

Be Fair

* Take turns
* Raise your hand
* Share

Be Respectful

* Use kind words
* Listen to others
* Take care of school supplies

Be Safe

* Walk; don't run
* Be careful

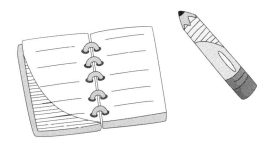

Name _____

Rules Graphic Organizer

What do people do here?

What rules make things fair?

Rules for

_____

What rules make things safe?

What rules show respect?

Name _____

Playground Rules Writing Task #1

Pretend that you are on the playground. Write rules that make playtime fair and safe.

Restaurant Rules Writing Task #2

Pretend that your family is going out to eat dinner. Write rules to follow so everyone has a good time.

😎 Extension Activity

Think of a game or an activity that you like to do. Write the rules for it.

Here's How

There are all kinds of directions. There are travel directions, telling someone how to find their way. There are directions for using devices, appliances, and machines. Directions help someone learn a new process. Games come with directions, too. A recipe is a set of directions to prepare food. Adults give directions to children to teach them basic living skills.

There are many ways to give directions to others. Directions can range from a simple one-sentence command to a whole technical manual. Sometimes we tell directions to someone who is helping us do something, such as cleaning up after lunch. Often we write them down so someone can refer back to them as needed. Sometimes directions need to include pictures or a map.

Written directions should contain the following:
- a goal or an objective to accomplish
- any materials needed
- clear steps written in order
- a description of what each step will look like, do, or make
- diagrams or pictures, if appropriate

The Lesson

Introduce: Using the information above, explain to students what different kinds of directions there are. Then distribute a copy of page 40 to each student. Read the scenario to students. Discuss it, asking students what kinds of things they have explained to others how to do.

Look at a Model: Read the model writing sample, "How to Play Hopscotch," to students. Discuss it, asking students if they could follow the directions. Ask students how much the picture helps. Ask whether they think anything could be added or changed in the directions.

Analyze the Model: Distribute a copy of the graphic organizer on page 41 to each student. Guide students through finding the information in the model writing sample to complete the graphic organizer. Some parts of the graphic organizer may not apply.

Write: Assign and provide copies of one or both writing tasks on pages 42 and 43 to students or allow them to choose. Also provide copies of the graphic organizer to help them plan their writing. Read the directions to students to make sure they understand the task. Then have students write their directions.

Extend: If desired, have students brainstorm situations in their own lives in which writing directions may be useful. Have them complete the extension activity on page 43 on a separate sheet of paper.

Different Ways to Play

Paul lives in Texas. He likes school. At recess, he loves to play games. His favorite game is called hopscotch.

Today, Paul talked to his Aunt Marie in France. He told her about school. Aunt Marie played hopscotch, too. But the game was different in France when she was young. Paul explained how he plays hopscotch in Texas.

How to Play Hopscotch

First, get some chalk and draw 10 squares on the sidewalk. Sometimes you can draw two squares together.

Second, number each square in order.

Third, toss a small rock onto square 1.

Fourth, hop in each square in order. Skip the square with the rock. Land on both feet when there are two squares together. Turn around and hop back. Pick up the rock when you come to it.

Do the same thing for the rest of the numbers.

Name _____

Directions Graphic Organizer

How to _____

Step 1

Step 2

Step 3

Step 4

What You Need

Name _____

Pet-Sitter Writing Task #1

Pretend that your friend will be feeding your cat while you are away from home. Write directions to tell your friend what to do.

How to Feed Fluffy

First, wash the cat's bowls.

LAP!
LAP!
LAP!

Name _____

Library Book Writing Task #2

Pretend that a new boy in class does not know how to check out a book from the classroom library. Write directions to tell him how.

😎 Extension Activity

Think of a real task that you need to explain to someone. Write directions for doing it.

Paint a Portrait with Words

We describe people all the time. Maybe someone wants to know what your best friend is like or who your teacher is. Usually we think of describing how people look, from their hair and skin color to their age, height, and weight. You might also describe how someone tends to dress or wear their hair, or mention any other distinctive style.

Think also about how people act: Are they relaxed or nervous? Are they talkative or shy? Do they look friendly or mean? Do they speak loudly or quietly, with confidence or humor? There are many ways we can tell people apart. The goal is to allow the listener to feel as if he or she knows the person you are describing.

A description of a person should contain the following:

- the person's name
- the person's relationship to the writer
- what the person looks like
- the person's personality
- sensory details
- the writer's feelings about the person

The Lesson

Introduce: Using the information above, explain to students what a description is. Then distribute a copy of page 45 to each student. Read the scenario to students. Discuss it, asking volunteers to share any similar experiences with a new member of the family.

Look at a Model: Read the model writing sample, "Dear Ms. Stanton," to students. Talk about the kinds of details being described. Ask how the details help readers form a picture in their mind.

Analyze the Model: Distribute a copy of the graphic organizer on page 46 to each student. Guide students through finding the information in the model writing sample to complete the graphic organizer. Some parts of the graphic organizer may not apply.

Write: Assign copies of one or both writing tasks on pages 47 and 48 to students or allow them to choose. Also provide copies of the graphic organizer to help them plan their writing. Read all the directions to students to make sure they understand the task. Then have students write their descriptions.

Extend: If desired, have students brainstorm other people they might want to describe. Have them complete the extension activity on page 48 on a separate sheet of paper.

Oh, Baby!

Estela has a new little brother. He was born over the summer. Estela is excited about being a big sister. She wrote a note to tell her teacher all about him.

Dear Ms. Stanton,

I am a big sister! I have a baby brother, and his name is Henry. He is soft and tiny. He has red hair like me. He sleeps a lot, but he cries at night. That's okay. I love my little brother!

Yours truly,
Estela

Name _____

Description Graphic Organizer

Meet _____,

my _____.

What _____ looks like

How _____ acts

How I feel about _____

Name _____

My Friend Writing Task #1

Describe your best friend. What is special about him or her? Write your description. Then draw a picture of your friend in the frame.

Community Helper Writing Task #2

Think of a community helper or school worker. Write a description of that person.

😎 Extension Activity

Your parents are going to a meeting at your school. They have never met your teacher. Write a description of your teacher so they can find him or her at the meeting.

Here's What I Think

Before the Internet, only professional critics wrote reviews of books and movies. Now, anyone can write a review, even students. Students' reviews help let their peers know whether a book, TV show, or movie is worth their time. Students trust the opinion of someone who is just like them. After all, who better to review children's entertainment than a child?

Many reviewers use a quick thumbs-up or thumbs-down symbol to indicate their opinion, but there could be many reasons for the opinion. Were the characters interesting? Was the story boring? Did the storyteller make you feel like you wanted to live in the setting? Did you learn anything from the story? The more information the review provides, the more helpful it will be.

A book or a movie review should contain the following:

- the name of the book, TV show, or movie you are reviewing
- a few sentences saying what the story is about
- your opinion
- details of what you liked or didn't like
- supporting details
- a thumbs-up or thumbs-down rating

The Lesson

Introduce: Using the information above, explain to students what a book, show, or movie review is. Then distribute a copy of page 50 to each student. Read the scenario to students. Ask students how they choose which books they want. Ask them if they are familiar with the book that the student is writing about.

Look at a Model: Read the model writing sample, "The Day the Crayons Quit," to students. Talk about the reasons that Roma gives to support her book choice. Discuss whether they are strong reasons.

Analyze the Model: Distribute a copy of the graphic organizer on page 51 to each student. Guide students through finding the information in the model writing sample to complete the graphic organizer. Some parts of the graphic organizer may not apply.

Write: Assign and provide copies of one or both writing tasks on pages 52 and 53 to students or allow them to choose. Also provide copies of the graphic organizer to help them plan their writing. Read all the directions to students to make sure they understand the task. Then have students write their reviews.

Extend: If desired, have students brainstorm books they have read in class. Have them complete the extension activity on page 53 on a separate sheet of paper.

Our Growing Library

Roma's class wants more books to read. The Parent Club will buy some. Roma wrote a review of a book. She wants the Parent Club to buy it for the class.

The Day the Crayons Quit

In this story, a boy likes to color. One day, he opens his crayon box. He finds a surprise. Some colors are tired of working. Some don't like being ignored. So they all quit. The boy has to solve the problem so he can color. The story is funny. I also liked the crayon drawings. <u>The Day the Crayons Quit</u> is a fun book. Our class library needs it.

Book and Show Review Graphic Organizer

Title—What I'm reviewing

What happens in the story

What I like

What I don't like

Would others like it?

Thumbs-up! Writing Task #1

Think of a show or a movie that you liked. What did you like about it? Write a review. Make a drawing to tell about it.

My review of _____

by _____

drawing

Thumbs-down! Writing Task #2

Think of a book or a show that you **didn't** like.
Why didn't you like it? Write a review.

My review of _____

by _____

😎 Extension Activity

Your friend is going to the library to look for a good book. Choose a book for your friend. Write a review of it.

What I Prefer

Everyone has opinions about food. You may not agree with someone's opinion, and that is fine. Tastes vary from person to person. Tastes can also vary from one year to another. For example, someone may have grown up disliking olives, and then one day discovers they are delicious in a Greek salad or in olive bread. Opinions often change as people grow and encounter new things.

When you express an opinion, it is important to support it with reasons. Repeating your opinion or stating it in a different way isn't the same as giving a reason. Clear reasons help readers understand your thoughts. You might even be able to change the reader's mind!

An opinion should contain the following:

- a topic sentence
- reasons
- signal words, such as *the best, I think,* or *I believe*
- describing words
- a conclusion
- a graphic related to the opinion, if needed

The Lesson

Introduce: Using the information above, explain to students what an opinion is. Then distribute a copy of page 55 to each student. Read the scenario to students. Talk about different vegetables that students like and dislike, focusing on their reasons why.

Look at a Model: Read the model writing sample, "Milo's Opinion," to students. Talk about the describing words and signal words that Milo uses to share his opinion. Help students identify the reasons Milo gives, and differentiate reason words from his opinion words.

Analyze the Model: Distribute a copy of the graphic organizer on page 56 to each student. Guide students through finding the information in the model writing sample to complete the graphic organizer. Some parts of the graphic organizer may not apply.

Write: Assign and provide copies of one or both writing tasks on pages 57 and 58 to students or allow them to choose. Also provide copies of the graphic organizer to help them plan their writing. Read all the directions to students to make sure they understand the task. Then have students write their opinions.

Extend: If desired, have students brainstorm desserts, good and bad, that they might write about. Have them complete the extension activity on page 58 on a separate sheet of paper.

The Worst Vegetable

Milo likes most vegetables. But he doesn't like Brussels sprouts. He wrote his opinion about them.

Milo's Opinion

I like most veggies, but I don't like Brussels sprouts. First, they taste bad to me. Second, I think they smell bad in the pan. When Mom cooks them, I go outside. Third, they make my stomach hurt. Fourth, they are slimy. I think I'm eating a big round worm! I believe Brussels sprouts are the worst veggie ever.

Name _____

Food Opinion Graphic Organizer

Opinion about _____

Reasons

Conclusion

Weekly Real-World Writing • EMC 6077 • © Evan-Moor Corp.

The Yummiest Fruit Writing Task #1

What fruit tastes the best to you? Write reasons for your opinion.
Make a drawing of the fruit in the bowl.

_____ tastes best because

Best Breakfast Writing Task #2

What breakfast do you like best? Write it on the menu. Then write why.

My Menu

Why I think it is the best:

Extension Activity

What is a dessert that you **don't** like? Write reasons for your opinion.

My Opinion Counts!

We can find reviews about practically anything online and in print: "I really liked the soup!" "These shoes are very comfortable!" "This toy broke after two weeks." When we write a review, we want to give others enough detail to make their own better-informed decisions.

The first thing that a reader of a review will notice is the rating, usually given in stars, a number, or thumbs-up/thumbs-down. The rating quickly and graphically shows praise, criticism, or a combination of both. The reader will want to know the reason for the rating, as well as whether the reviewer recommends the product.

A product review should contain the following:

- a title and the writer's name
- the name of the product
- the purpose of the product
- opinion statements
- supporting details
- the reviewer's rating of the product

The Lesson

Introduce: Using the information above, explain to students what a product review is. Then distribute a copy of page 60 to each student. Read the scenario to students. Discuss it, asking students how they feel about new items they receive. Do they always like them? Are they always fun to play with? Do toys always work? Do clothes always fit?

Look at a Model: Read the model writing sample, "It's Fun to Watch!" to students. Talk about the star rating. Discuss some possible reasons for **not** liking the ant farm. How many stars might Carmela have given if it was broken, hard to see the ants, or not easy to set up?

Analyze the Model: Distribute a copy of the graphic organizer on page 61 to each student. Guide students through finding the information in the model writing sample to complete the graphic organizer. Some parts of the graphic organizer may not apply.

Write: Assign and provide copies of one or both writing tasks on pages 62 and 63 to students or allow them to choose. Also provide copies of the graphic organizer to help them plan their writing. Read all the directions to students to make sure they understand the task. Then have students write their reviews.

Extend: If desired, have students brainstorm other toys they might want to review. Have them complete the extension activity on page 63 on a separate sheet of paper.

How Many Stars?

Carmela's uncle gave Carmela an ant farm. Then they set up the ant farm. Carmela watches the ants every day. Carmela wrote a review of the Sandy Hill Ant Farm.

It's Fun to Watch!

Carmela B.

My uncle gave me this ant farm. My mom and I set up the ant farm. The ants are alive! We put everything in the ant farm. In one day, the ants made many tunnels. The ants are under the sand, but the sides are clear so you can see them. I love watching the ants do their work.

I will take my ant farm to school for show and tell. Everyone will like this ant farm!

Sandy Hill Ant Farm

Name _____

Product Review Graphic Organizer

Name of item: _____

Why I got it: _____

_____

What I **like** about it: _____

_____

What I **don't like** about it: _____

_____

Why: _____

_____

My rating: ☆ ☆ ☆ ☆ ☆

Should readers buy it? Circle: YES   NO

Summer Splash Writing Task #1

Toby got a small kiddie pool and filled it with water. He played all day.
Pretend that you are Toby. Write a review of the pool. Give a rating.

My review of _____

by _____

☆ ☆ ☆ ☆ ☆

Name _____

Toy Farm Writing Task #2

Lia had fun at her grandparents' farm. They sent her a toy farm with horses, cows, and sheep. It had some wood sticks to make a fence and a barn. Pretend that you are Lia. Write a review of the farm. Give a rating.

My review of _____

by _____

😎 **Extension Activity**

Think of a toy that you recently played with. Write a review of it.

Weather and Climate

What do you think of winter? People who live in mild climates might welcome winter because that is when it rains and everything turns green. Some people may love winter sports. But those who endure long bitter-cold winters may not feel the same. It is hard to travel anywhere on snowy or icy roads. The same goes for summer. Some people enjoy swimming and dressing lightly, while others are so hot that they can't think. Feelings about weather and climate vary, depending on location and lifestyle.

Whatever your opinion may be about the weather or climate, it is important to support it with reasons—whether you like rain or sun!

An opinion should contain the following:
- a topic sentence
- reasons
- signal words such as *better, best,* or *more*
- descriptive words
- a conclusion
- a graphic related to the opinion, if needed

The Lesson

Introduce: Using the information above, explain to students what an opinion is. Then distribute a copy of page 65 to each student. Read the scenario to students. Have students describe winter and summer and what students do where you live. Ask students which season they prefer and why.

Look at a Model: Read the model writing sample, "Rico's Opinion," to students. Talk about the describing words and signal words that Rico uses to describe his preferred season. Help students identify the reasons Rico gives, and differentiate them from his opinion.

Analyze the Model: Distribute a copy of the graphic organizer on page 66 to each student. Guide students through finding the information in the model writing sample to complete the graphic organizer. Some parts of the graphic organizer may not apply.

Write: Assign and provide copies of one or both writing tasks on pages 67 and 68 to students or allow them to choose. Also provide copies of the graphic organizer to help them plan their writing. Read all the directions to students to make sure they understand the task. Then have students write their opinions.

Extend: If desired, have students think about other kinds of weather to write about. Have them complete the extension activity on page 68 on a separate sheet of paper.

Hot or Cold?

Rico lives in Chicago. Summers are very hot. Winters are very cold. He thinks about what he likes to do. Rico wrote about which season he likes better.

Rico's Opinion

Where I live, winters are cold. I can't go outside when it is too cold. That's why I like summer more. It is very hot, but I get to swim in the fun pool. I can eat cold ice cream. I like to wear cool shorts. This is why summer is better than winter.

Name _____

Weather Opinion Graphic Organizer

I like _____ more than _____ .

What I like about

_____

What I don't like about

_____

Rain or Shine? Writing Task #1

Which do you like **less**, a rainy day or a sunny day?
Give reasons for your opinion. Make a drawing.

I don't like a _____

day as much as a _____

day because

Best Season Writing Task #2

Draw a picture of yourself in your favorite season. Write why you like it.

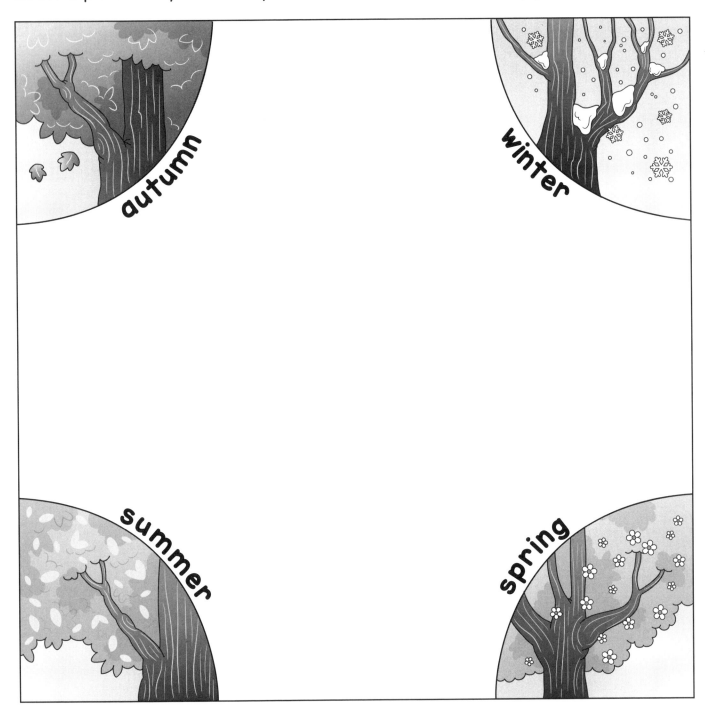

😎 Extension Activity

What are the best and worst things about wind? Write your opinion.

Where Do I Come From?

When we ask ourselves "Where do I come from?" it often includes finding out where our family lived before they arrived where they are now. While genetic testing might give people more geographic clues about their ancestry, it can't explain *why* they lived where they did or *what* brought them to where they are now. The best way to learn interesting stories about family or culture is to ask the oldest family members about their lives. By asking the right questions, we can hear a wealth of family adventures.

An **interview** is a conversation between two people in which one person asks questions and the other answers them. Everyone has a unique perspective and different experiences. Interviews help readers better understand others and let us see the world through their eyes.

Family-history interviews should contain questions about the following:

- when and where the person was born
- the history of the person's name
- favorite things the person did as a child
- the person's childhood home
- any marriages
- family traditions

The Lesson

Introduce: Using the information above, explain to students what an interview is. Then distribute a copy of page 70 to each student. Read the scenario to students. Discuss possible reasons that Bella might not know her grandfather.

Look at a Model: Read the model writing sample, "Dear Grandma Isabella," to students. Discuss it, asking students what they think about the questions. Ask if they have any older relatives or relatives who live far away whom they have never met. Ask whether they think anything could be added or changed to improve the e-mail interview.

Analyze the Model: Distribute a copy of the graphic organizer on page 71 to each student. Guide students through finding the information in the model writing sample to complete the graphic organizer. Some parts of the graphic organizer may not apply.

Write: Assign and provide copies of one or both writing tasks on pages 72 and 73 to students or allow them to choose. Also provide copies of the graphic organizer to help them plan their writing. Read all the directions to students to make sure they understand the task. Then have students write their interview questions.

Extend: If desired, have students discuss how older family members may have contributed to their community. Have them complete the extension activity on page 73 on a separate sheet of paper.

Grandpa Marco

Bella was named after her grandmother. Bella loves her Grandma Isabella, but she never got to meet her grandfather. She has seen pictures of him, but she doesn't know much about him. Bella e-mailed her grandmother to find out more about Grandpa Marco.

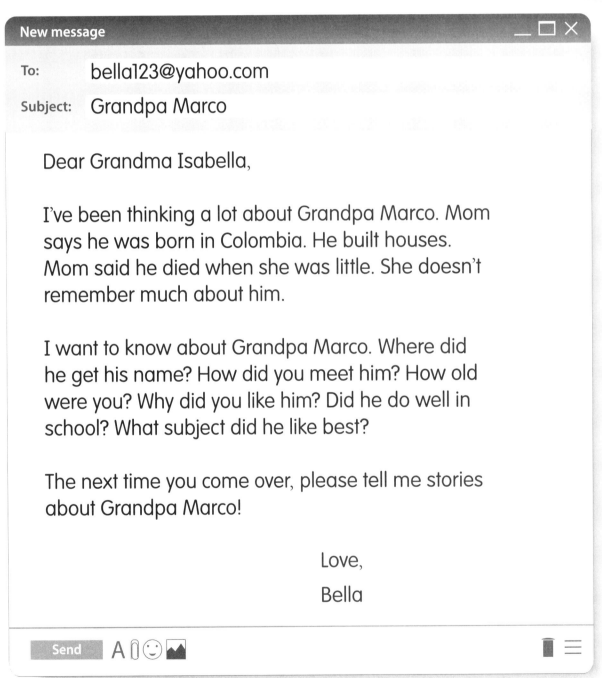

New message   _ □ ✕

To: bella123@yahoo.com

Subject: Grandpa Marco

Dear Grandma Isabella,

I've been thinking a lot about Grandpa Marco. Mom says he was born in Colombia. He built houses. Mom said he died when she was little. She doesn't remember much about him.

I want to know about Grandpa Marco. Where did he get his name? How did you meet him? How old were you? Why did you like him? Did he do well in school? What subject did he like best?

The next time you come over, please tell me stories about Grandpa Marco!

Love,

Bella

Send   A ᵢ ☺ 🖼

Name _____

Interview Graphic Organizer

Questions about
the person's home

Questions about
things the person did

Questions about
who the person lived with

Questions about
family traditions

At My Age Writing Task #1

Choose an older family member to interview. Find out what he or she was like at your age. Use question words to write questions to learn about his or her childhood friends, school, pets, or favorite toys.

Question Words

| Who | What | Where | When | Why | How | Did |

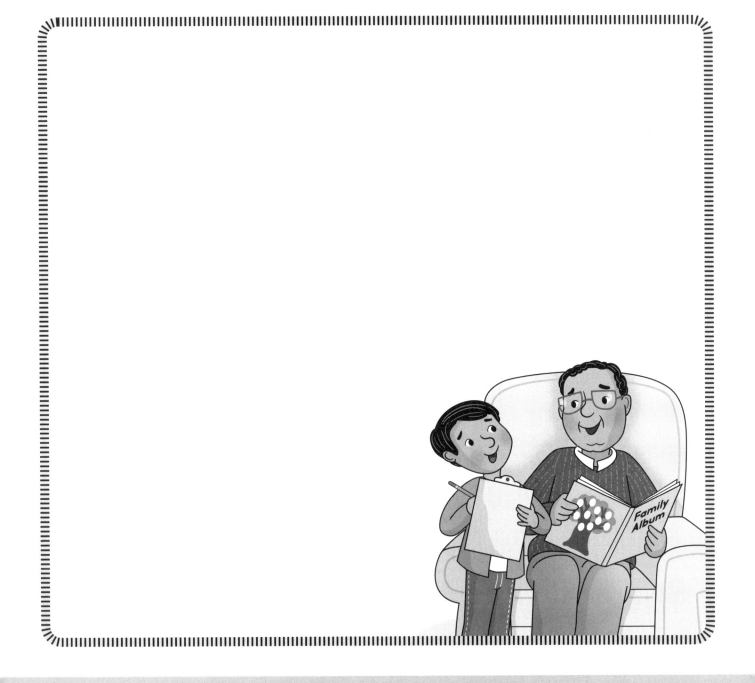

Family Names Writing Task #2

Choose someone in your family to interview about your name. Ask how your first name was chosen. Ask if your last name means anything. Find out about naming traditions in your family, too.

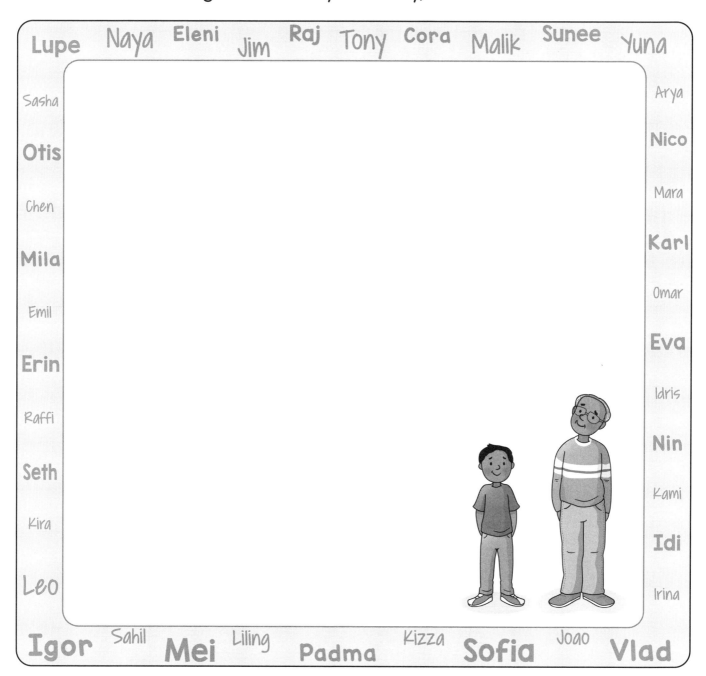

😎 Extension Activity

Interview someone to find out if there are any famous people in your family.

Doctor, Doctor!

It is very important to take care of our health. When we don't feel good, we can't do things that we want or need to do. Our bodies have a lot of moving parts inside. Most of the time, we can ignore those parts. We just eat when we're hungry, sleep when we're tired, and bandage cuts and scrapes. Doctors can help us with any other problems. But we might have health questions that come up when we are not in a doctor's office. Then we can do an Internet search to find answers.

Online health information is nearly always written for adults, so teachers and parents may have to "translate" medical information for students. But it is never too early for students to start asking health questions and learning to use online resources.

An Internet search question should contain the following:

- precise words about body parts or illnesses
- a specific question stating what you want to know
- a short phrase that is likely to appear in a search result

The Lesson

Introduce: Using the information above, explain to students what an Internet search is. Then distribute a copy of page 75 to each student. Read the scenario to students. Explain where the tonsils are located. Ask if anyone has had their tonsils removed or any other operation.

Look at a Model: Read the model writing sample, "Learning More," to students. Point out that a search can be a single word, a phrase, or a complete sentence or question. Discuss the types of words that are most important in a search. Show on an actual device where the search words should be typed. Ask whether students think anything could be added or changed to improve the Internet search.

Analyze the Model: Distribute a copy of the graphic organizer on page 76 to each student. Guide students through finding the information in the model writing sample to complete the graphic organizer. Some parts of the graphic organizer may not apply.

Write: Assign and provide copies of one or both writing tasks on pages 77 and 78 to students or allow them to choose. Also provide copies of the graphic organizer to help them plan their writing. Read all the directions to students to make sure they understand the task. Then have students write their search words and questions.

Extend: If desired, have students brainstorm health-related topics they would like to know about. Have them complete the extension activity on page 78 on a separate sheet of paper.

Tina's Tonsils

Tommy has a little sister named Tina. Tina's throat hurts when she swallows. The problem is Tina's tonsils. Her doctor wants to take out her tonsils. The operation is called a **tonsillectomy**.

Tommy wonders how the doctor will get the tonsils out of Tina's throat. He wonders if it will hurt. He wonders how fast she will get better after the operation. So Tommy did an Internet search.

Learning More

Search...

tonsils

tonsillectomy

Does it hurt to have tonsils taken out?

What happens after your tonsils are gone?

getting better after an operation

Name _____

Internet Search Graphic Organizer

What do you want to know?

_____

_____

_____

_____

What could the answers be?

_____

_____

_____

_____

What are the most important words you wrote above?

_____	_____
_____	_____
_____	_____

Name _____

Broken Arm Writing Task #1

Pretend that your friend broke his arm. You write your name on his cast. You want to find out more about casts and broken bones. Write words and questions for an Internet search.

Search...

[blank field]

[blank field]

[blank field]

[blank field]

Name _____

Black and Blue Writing Task #2

Pretend that you are playing ball. A ball hits your leg. Ouch! Your skin turns red where the ball hit. Later, it turns into a black-and-blue bruise. You want to know why your skin changed color. Write words and questions for an Internet search.

Search...

Extension Activity

What do you wonder about your health? Write words and questions for an Internet search.

Getting to Know You

When we meet new people, we want to find out all about them. Sometimes we meet them in person: they move to a new neighborhood and start attending a new school, a club, a team, or a place of worship. Sometimes we meet them online: they join our social media, vlog, or other virtual sphere. Either way, we need to find out what they are like.

The Internet has brought the world to our fingertips. We can meet pen pals on the other side of the globe and share different cultures, different ways of living, different viewpoints, and different ways to solve problems. All we have to do is ask!

A letter, an e-mail, or a text to a new friend should contain the following:
- questions about where he or she lives or comes from and age or grade
- questions about what he or she likes about school
- questions about favorite things (food, color, toy, pet, hobbies)
- questions that start with *why* or *how*
- friendly and polite wording
- emojis and colorful fonts, if desired

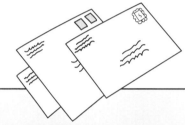

The Lesson

Introduce: Using the information above, explain to students how a letter to someone new is different from a letter to someone you know. Then distribute a copy of page 80 to each student. Read the scenario to students. Discuss it, asking students where and how they meet new friends. Ask if anyone has ever had a pen pal.

Look at a Model: Read the model writing sample, "Dear Holly," to students. Talk about the questions Yuna asked in the e-mail. Ask students why each one is interesting and what the answer tells you. Ask whether they think anything could be added or changed in the e-mail.

Analyze the Model: Distribute a copy of the graphic organizer on page 81 to each student. The graphic organizer gives sentence starters using common question words, but there are many other ways to start a question. Guide students through finding the information in the model writing sample to complete the graphic organizer. Some sentence starters in the graphic organizer may not apply.

Write: Assign and provide copies of one or both writing tasks on pages 82 and 83 to students or allow them to choose. Also provide copies of the graphic organizer to help them plan their writing. Read all the directions to students to make sure they understand the task. Then have students write their friendly messages.

Extend: If desired, have students brainstorm situations in their own lives in which they moved to a new town, started going to a new school, or joined a new class, a team, or another group and wanted to make new friends. Have them complete the extension activity on page 83 on a separate sheet of paper.

Yuna Gets a Pen Pal

Yuna's teacher gave each student in class a pen pal. A pen pal is someone who lives far away. Pen pals write to each other to become friends. Yuna's pen pal, Holly, lives in England. She wrote her first e-mail to Holly.

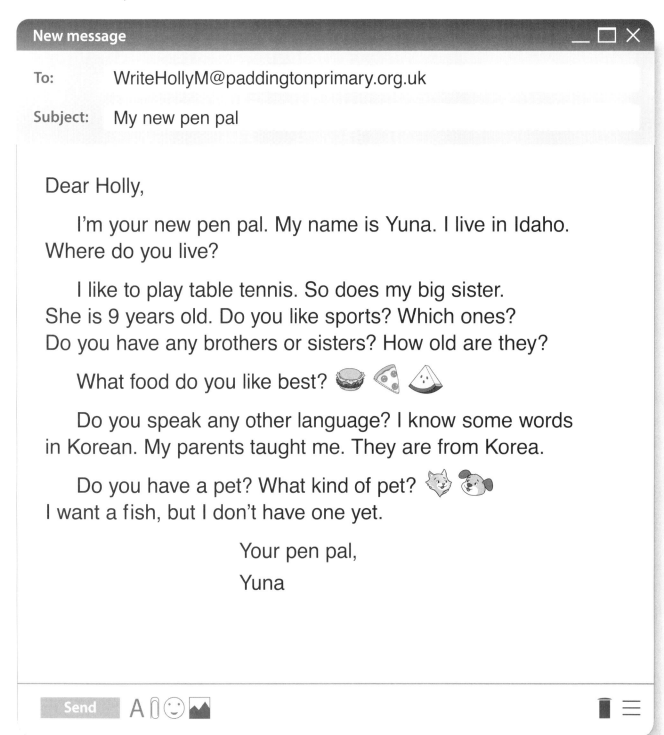

New message _ ▢ ✕

To: WriteHollyM@paddingtonprimary.org.uk

Subject: My new pen pal

Dear Holly,

I'm your new pen pal. My name is Yuna. I live in Idaho. Where do you live?

I like to play table tennis. So does my big sister. She is 9 years old. Do you like sports? Which ones? Do you have any brothers or sisters? How old are they?

What food do you like best?

Do you speak any other language? I know some words in Korean. My parents taught me. They are from Korea.

Do you have a pet? What kind of pet? I want a fish, but I don't have one yet.

Your pen pal,

Yuna

Send A ◖ ☺ ◩

New-Friend Letter Graphic Organizer

Ask **where** something happens.

Where did _____?

Ask **when** something happens.

When did _____?

Ask **who** does something.

Who can _____?

Ask **what** something is.

What is _____?

Ask **why** something happens.

Why does _____?

Ask **do** questions.

Do you like _____?

Name _____

Message Board Writing Task #1

Pretend that you go to class online. You and your classmates see the teacher and each other on a computer screen. This week, a new student named Zane joined the class. Your teacher, Mr. Murthy, wants Zane to feel at home in his new class. Send Zane questions on the class message board.

Dear Camper Writing Task #2

Pretend that your family went camping. Another family at the campground had a child your age. You had fun together. Write him or her a letter. Tell him or her about your life at home.

😎 Extension Activity

Think of a time when you were new to a town, a class, or a group. Write a letter or an e-mail to someone you met.

Curiosity and Inquiry

What makes the wind blow? How do leaves change color? Why can birds fly but ants can't? What would happen if nothing ever died? Cultivating questions like these capitalizes on students' sense of wonder. Student-generated questions open the mind to exploration. These types of questions may be answered by different kinds of scientists, but they can also be explored by observation and active investigation.

In order to learn how the natural world works, students start by asking thoughtful questions. Each question should focus on a particular phenomenon. Sometimes the answers inspire more questions. Investigation can inspire "What if" questions about the effects of specific conditions. Inquiry opens the door to learning.

A science question should contain the following:

- an observation of the natural world based on a sense
- question words such as *where, when, why, what,* or *how*
- friendly and polite wording
- pictures, if needed

The Lesson

Introduce: Using the information above, explain to students what science questions are and how they are different from conversational questions. Then distribute a copy of page 85 to each student. Read the scenario to students. Discuss what a drought is and ask if they have ever experienced a long time without rain.

Look at a Model: Read the model writing sample, "A Bunch of Questions," to students. Discuss it, asking students why Dan has all these questions. Ask if they think Uncle Ray is a good person to ask and why. Are Dan's questions asking for opinions or information? Ask if anything should be added or changed in the questions.

Analyze the Model: Distribute a copy of the graphic organizer on page 86 to each student. Guide students through finding the information in the model writing sample to complete the graphic organizer. Some parts of the graphic organizer may not apply.

Write: Assign and provide copies of both writing tasks on pages 87 and 88 to students or allow them to choose. Also provide copies of the graphic organizer to help them plan their writing. Read all the directions to students to make sure they understand the task. Then have students write their questions.

Extend: If desired, teach students how to play the game Animal, Vegetable, or Mineral. Brainstorm examples of things in each group. Model the question-and-answer process. Have them complete the extension activity on page 88.

Dry Land

It hasn't rained in a very long time where Dan lives. The grass in his town is all brown and plants are dying. Dan learned that this long dry spell is called a **drought**.

Dan has questions about the drought. He knows it has something to do with water. He wrote an e-mail to his uncle, who is a water scientist.

A Bunch of Questions

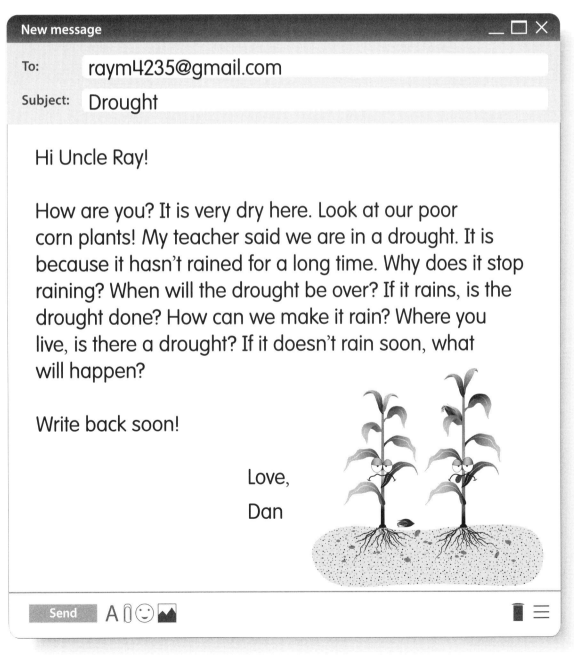

New message

To: raym4235@gmail.com

Subject: Drought

Hi Uncle Ray!

How are you? It is very dry here. Look at our poor corn plants! My teacher said we are in a drought. It is because it hasn't rained for a long time. Why does it stop raining? When will the drought be over? If it rains, is the drought done? How can we make it rain? Where you live, is there a drought? If it doesn't rain soon, what will happen?

Write back soon!

Love,

Dan

Send

Science Questions Graphic Organizer

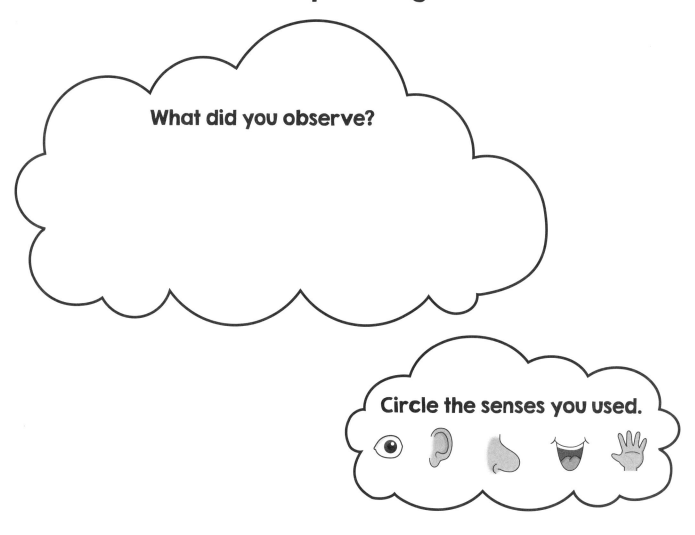

What did you observe?

Circle the senses you used.

What do you want to know about? _____

Circle a question word:

When   Where   Why   What   How   Can   Do   Is

Write your question: _____

_____

Can it be answered by   ☐ asking a scientist?
                          ☐ a science book or the Internet?
                          ☐ doing science?

Ask Sana Writing Task #1

A space scientist named Sana studies the night sky. She has a website called "Sana's Skies." It has information, photos, and games. It also lets children ask questions about the moon, stars, and planets. What questions would you ask?

Sana's Skies

Ask Sana

Write your questions here!

Become a Weather Pal Writing Task #2

A local TV news station invites students to ask about weather, such as snow, thunder, lightning, or rainbows. They draw a picture and send it with their question. The station answers the questions on TV. Think of a question about weather. Write and draw it on the Weather Pal form.

Weather Pal

Name: _____ Age: _____

Write your question:

Draw your weather:

Extension Activity

Play the game Animal, Vegetable, or Mineral with friends. Think of something in one of these groups. Say, "I am thinking of something in the _____ group." Your friends ask questions that can be answered **yes** or **no**. The first person to guess what you are thinking of goes next.

Making Choices

Sometimes, making decisions is easy, especially if you have a favorite. But often, decisions are difficult, especially if no choice is perfect. You sometimes choose between doing something or not doing it, such as sharing something with someone. For example, you may be enjoying eating your favorite cookies, but sharing your cookies might help someone who looks sad. Each option often has reasons for doing it and reasons against doing it. You sometimes choose between two things, such as what to wear today. For example, your sandals are more comfortable, but your boots are better if it rains.

One tool to help decide between options is a pro-and-con list. With young children, you may wish to call it a "choice list." When you analyze and list the good and bad things, the best choice is often clear.

A choice list should contain the following:

- what you are trying to decide
- a *Yes* column for writing the good things
- a *No* column for writing the bad things
- a word or a picture for each reason

The Lesson

Introduce: Using the information above, explain to students what a choice list is. Then distribute a copy of page 90 to each student. Read the scenario to students. Discuss it, asking students if they have ever thought about getting a pet or asked their parents for something important. Call attention to the parent's reasons for not wanting a pet.

Look at a Model: Read the model writing sample, "Should I get a dog?" to students. Point out the structure of the choice list: the question, two columns, and reasons. Then have them illustrate each column. Discuss the choice list, asking students how they would decide. Ask whether they think anything could be added or changed in the list.

Analyze the Model: Distribute a copy of the graphic organizer on page 91 to each student. Guide students through finding the information in the model writing sample to complete the graphic organizer. Some parts of the graphic organizer may not apply.

Write: Assign and provide copies of one or both writing tasks on pages 92 and 93 to students or allow them to choose. Also provide copies of the graphic organizer to help them plan their writing. Read all the directions to students to make sure they understand the task. Then have students complete their choice lists.

Extend: If desired, have students brainstorm situations in their own lives in which writing a choice list may be useful. Have them complete the extension activity on page 93 on a separate sheet of paper.

A Little Puppy

Pat likes dogs. He wants to get one. His mom does not. She said that dogs need care. They are a lot of work. Mom does not have time.

So Pat made a choice list. First, he wrote why he should get a dog. Then he wrote why he should not get a dog.

Should I get a dog?

Yes 👍	No 👎
Dogs like to play.	Dogs get dirty.
We can go on walks.	Dogs make a mess.
Dogs keep you warm.	Dogs jump on things.
You can hug and pet dogs.	Dogs bark.
	Dogs chew slippers.
	Dogs chase cars.
	Dogs bite people.

Name _____

Choice List Graphic Organizer

Should I _____ ?

Yes	No

Name _____

Play Ball Writing Task #1

Pretend that you can join a baseball team.

Make a choice list to help you decide.

Should I join the baseball team?

Yes	No

Weekly Real-World Writing • EMC 6077 • © Evan-Moor Corp.

Name _____

Share a Room Writing Task #2

Pretend that you have to decide if you want to share a room with your brother or sister. Make a choice list to help you decide.

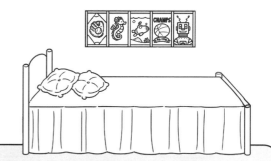

Should I share a room?	
Yes	No

😎 Extension Activity

Pretend that your mom and dad ask if you want to move to a new house. It is bigger and near the train. Make a choice list to help you decide.

Confusing Critters

Quick! What just hopped across the field? Was it a rabbit or a hare? It might be hard to tell them apart, especially when they dart past you in the blink of an eye. It doesn't help that they're both furry and have long ears. They also behave in a similar manner. But did you know that a rabbit and a hare are not just different words for the same thing? In fact, they are completely different animals!

A rabbit and a hare are just one of many animal pairs that are often confused with one another. A good way to tell similar creatures apart is to look closely at their characteristics and compare them. For example, hares are larger than rabbits, and their fur changes color with the seasons. Hares run away to avoid danger, while rabbits hide. Hares eat tree bark and twigs, while rabbits eat grasses and vegetables. Hares make nests, while rabbits burrow underground. Writing comparisons helps you "see" differences more clearly.

 A comparison should contain the following:
- the names of the two similar things
- descriptions of what they look like
- descriptions of how they act
- descriptions of where they live
- pictures of each living thing

The Lesson

Introduce: Using the information above, explain to students what a comparison is. Then distribute a copy of page 95 to each student. Read the scenario to students. Ask students why Asad may have thought Nik's pet was a turtle. Ask if they know any differences between a turtle and a tortoise.

Look at a Model: Read the model writing sample, "What's the Difference?" to students. Brainstorm sources of information that Asad may have used in his search. Guide students to notice the types of descriptions he listed (physical, habitat, behavior).

Analyze the Model: Distribute a copy of the graphic organizer on page 96 to each student. Guide students through finding the information in the model writing sample to complete the graphic organizer. Some parts of the graphic organizer may not apply.

Write: Assign and provide copies of one or both writing tasks on pages 97 and 98 to students or allow them to choose. Also provide copies of the graphic organizer to help them plan their writing. Read all the directions to students to make sure they understand the task. Then have students write their comparisons.

Extend: If desired, have students brainstorm other commonly confused animals. Have them complete the extension activity on page 98 on a separate sheet of paper.

Nik's New Pet

Asad goes to his friend's home. His friend, Nik, has a new pet. "What a cool turtle!" Asad says.

Nik says, "It has a shell like a turtle, but this is a tortoise. Her name is Tao."

Asad wonders how a turtle and a tortoise are different. When he went home, he read about both of them.

PET STORE

What's the Difference?

Tortoise	Turtle

Tortoise	Turtle
rounded shell	flatter shell
lives on land	lives mostly in water
legs are thick and round	legs are flatter and webbed
eats only plants	eats plants, insects, and meat

Comparison Graphic Organizer

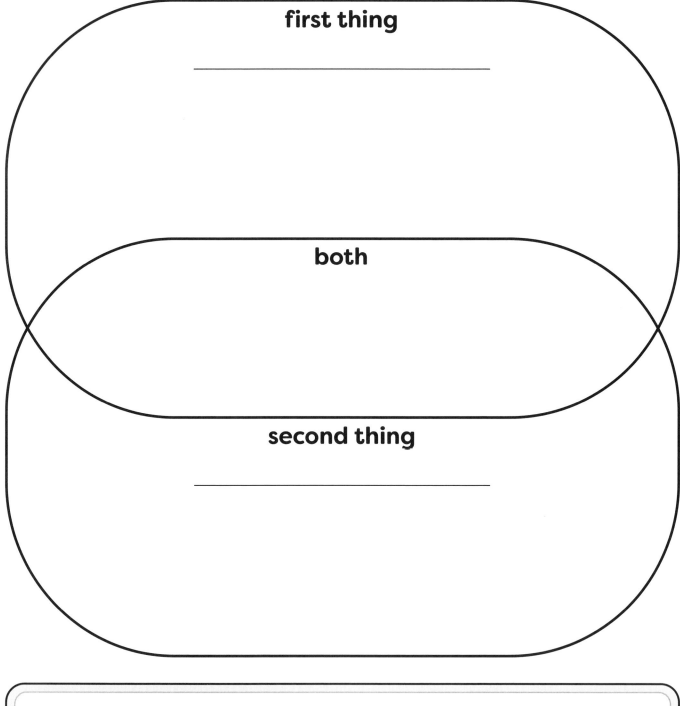

first thing

_____

both

second thing

_____

Some things to compare:

☐ size   ☐ where it is   ☐ parts it has

☐ color   ☐ what it does   ☐ how it moves

Name _____

Bees and Wasps Writing Task #1

Tiki and her mom were picking flowers. A flying insect stung Tiki's mom! Her ankle was red and puffy. "I think it was a bee," said Mom. Tiki thinks it was a wasp. What is the difference? Read about bees and wasps. Compare the two insects.

 bee

 wasp

Name _____

Seals and Sea Lions Writing Task #2

Jin and Lan are cousins. When Jin visits Lan at the beach, they see some animals lying on the rocks. "Look at all those seals!" Jin says.

"Those are sea lions. They're cousins of seals, like us!" says Lan. What is the difference? Read about seals and sea lions. Compare the two animals.

seal	sea lion

😎 Extension Activity

Think of animal pairs that look almost alike. Read about them if you need to. Write a comparison.

Nature Walk

Keeping a journal is a great way to record all the wondrous observations we make: things we see, smell, hear, and feel while we are in nature. The forest, river, park, and even the backyard are great places to slow down and take a closer look. You can take photos, make drawings, and pick up pieces of nature as long as it is not harming any living thing and you have permission.

Making an observation is useful for adding onto what we know. Observations even improve our safety. For example, if you are riding a bike, you might see or hear other vehicles. But if you are heading toward an intersection, you need to observe and take note of where cars, pedestrians, and other cyclists are, as well as traffic signs, to make sure you don't collide with them. Noting our observations is what makes us process them, pay attention to them, and think about what they indicate. Without that processing, what we sense will soon be forgotten.

A written observation should contain the following:

- the date
- descriptive language using the senses
- interactions between things
- drawings
- pieces of nature, if appropriate

The Lesson

Introduce: Using the information above, explain to students what an observation is. Then distribute a copy of page 100 to each student. Read the scenario to students. Have them discuss what it is like after a storm where they live: what they see, hear, smell, and feel.

Look at a Model: Read the model writing sample, "My Backyard," to students. Talk about each detail that Silvie recorded and how it added to the "word picture" of the whole storm.

Analyze the Model: Distribute a copy of the graphic organizer on page 101 to each student. Guide students through finding the information in the model writing sample to complete the graphic organizer. Some parts of the graphic organizer may not apply.

Write: Assign and provide copies of one or both writing tasks on pages 102 and 103 to students or allow them to choose. Also provide copies of the graphic organizer to help them plan their writing. Read all the directions to students to make sure they understand the task. Then have students write their observations.

Extend: If desired, have students tell about their favorite nature spots. Have them complete the extension activity on page 103 on a separate sheet of paper.

After the Storm

Silvie lives in Texas. After a thunderstorm, she explores her backyard. She sees the mess that the storm left behind. Silvie wrote her observations in her journal.

My Backyard

June 24

We had a big storm last night. Lots of rain hit my window. I was scared it would break. The noisy wind blew and blew. It broke a branch off our pecan tree. Look at all those wet pecans on the ground! Those nuts are not ready to eat. ☹

Observation Graphic Organizer

Nature Observation

Date: _____

Where are you?

_____

What is the weather like?

_____

👁 What do you see? _____

👂 What do you hear? _____

👃 What do you smell? _____

✋ What do you feel? _____

What will you draw or take a photo of?

_____

Name _____

Tree Details Writing Task #1

Find a tree that you really like. Observe its details and write about it.
Show your observations to a friend. See if your friend can find your tree.

Date:

What is its shape?

What is its bark like?

What shape are its leaves?

Describe any fruit, flowers, or cones on the tree.

What colors are on the tree?

Name _____

Nature in Motion Writing Task #2

Go exploring outside and find something that moves. It could be an animal or the wind blowing something. It could be something that is falling. Write about what is moving. Describe the motion.

What is moving?

Is it moving up, down, sideways, or in a circle?

How fast is it moving?

What is making it move?

Is the motion smooth or bumpy?

😎 Extension Activity

Find a place in nature. Write observations of that place during each season of the year.

The View from Different Angles

When we look at things closely, we see details that help us understand them better. But things have several different sides. The top of a tree looks different from the bottom of a tree. The front of a giraffe looks different from the back of a giraffe. The inside of a building looks different from the outside. Scientists need to understand the world around them, so they observe it from different perspectives. They make sketches or diagrams to record their findings.

Observation using all our senses is an important skill. So is documenting those observations. Words are important to explain much of what we observe, especially what we see, hear, feel, smell, taste, and know. But a picture is worth a thousand words, and a diagram can organize details at a glance.

Diagrams should contain the following:

- the name of the object or living thing
- words or pictures of its parts
- sensory descriptions
- a description of any changes observed
- drawings and labels of different views
- measurements or other data, if appropriate

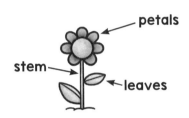

The Lesson

Introduce: Using the information above, explain to students what a diagram is. Then distribute a copy of page 105 to each student. Read the scenario to students. Ask students to describe apples that they have seen or eaten. How do they usually eat apples (whole, sliced, pieces, applesauce)?

Look at a Model: Read the model writing sample, "Apples Inside and Out," to students. Discuss it, asking students why Arpad had the apples cut open. How was the outside different from the inside? How did one side look different from the other side? What senses did he use?

Analyze the Model: Distribute a copy of the graphic organizer on page 106 to each student. Guide students through finding the information in the model writing sample to complete the graphic organizer. Some parts of the graphic organizer may not apply.

Write: Assign and provide copies of one or both writing tasks on pages 107 and 108 to students or allow them to choose. Also provide copies of the graphic organizer to help them plan their writing. Read all the directions to students to make sure they understand the task. Then have students make their diagrams.

Extend: If desired, have students brainstorm how they can observe and diagram different animals. Have them complete the extension activity on page 108 on a separate sheet of paper.

Picking Fruit

Arpad picked two shiny apples from his aunt's tree. He felt the smooth skin and smelled the sweet scent. He wanted to observe the apples carefully. He asked his aunt to cut them in two different ways. Arpad drew and labeled diagrams of what he saw.

Apples Inside and Out

	One View	Another View
Outside	My apple is smooth, shiny, and red. It smells sweet.	The other side has a worm hole!
Inside	seeds It is cut in half from top to bottom. It is light yellow and has seeds inside.	seeds It is cut in half across the middle. It is round, and the seeds make a star!

Name _____

Diagram Graphic Organizer

Observation Diagram

What I'm observing: _____

How I will look at it:

From different places

☐ from the **side**   ☐ from the **top**

☐ from the **front**   ☐ from the **bottom**

☐ from the **back**   ☐ from the **inside**

Using different senses

☐ What does it **look** like?   ☐ What does it **smell** like?

☐ What does it **feel** like?   ☐ What does it **taste** like?

☐ What does it **sound** like?

At different times

☐ in the **morning**   ☐ in the **evening**

☐ in the **afternoon**   ☐ at _____

What I will draw: _____

What I will label: _____

                Weekly Real-World Writing • EMC 6077 • © Evan-Moor Corp.

Name _____

Weather Watch Writing Task #1

What is the weather like today? Go outside in the morning, in the afternoon, and in the evening. Find the sun (but don't look right at it). What is in the air? Rain? Snow? Wind? Fog? Clouds? If you can, find out the temperature for each part of the day. Draw and write your observations to complete the diagram.

Today's Weather

	Where is the sun?	What is in the air?	How warm is it?
Morning			
Afternoon			
Evening			

Bird's-eye View Writing Task #2

Sit next to a flower or a plant and observe it. Draw a diagram of it. Label the parts. Then think of a bird flying above. How would the flower or plant look to the bird? Draw the flower or plant from the bird's view, looking down at it. Draw a diagram of it. Label the parts.

Diagrams from Two Views

Sitting next to it	
Flying over it	

😎 Extension Activity

Observe your favorite animal. Draw how it looks when it is still. Draw how it looks when it walks, runs, jumps, slides, swims, or flies. Label its parts. Write about how it sounds, feels, and smells.

Buy the Best

We are surrounded by advertisements—on television, on billboards, in print, online, and on signs. Buy One Get One Free! Everyone Needs This! Sale Starts Saturday! Going Fast! Everything that we buy is advertised: toys, games, foods, equipment, cars, clothing, and more.

Ads are probably the most common form of persuasive writing. One purpose of an ad is to inform people about a product. It might claim that the product has the best quality at the best price. The primary purpose, however, is to convince people to buy the product. The ad must make the product look and sound so good that readers can't resist buying it.

An advertisement should contain the following:

- the name of the product
- reasons to buy the product
- a picture of the product
- the price
- where to buy the product
- concise, catchy wording

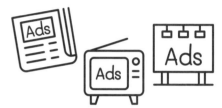

The Lesson

Introduce: Using the information above, explain to students what an advertisement, or an ad, is. Then distribute a copy of page 110 to each student. Read the scenario to students. Ask students how an ad will help Miguel sell lemonade. Ask about ads that students have seen around town.

Look at a Model: Read the model writing sample, "Fresh Lemonade!" to students. Discuss how the ad shows how the cut lemons and the word *fresh* make the lemonade seem tasty. What will people walking or driving by probably do when they see the ad? Ask students whether they think anything could be added or changed in the ad.

Analyze the Model: Distribute a copy of the graphic organizer on page 111 to each student. Guide students through finding the information in the model writing sample to complete the graphic organizer. Some parts of the graphic organizer may not apply.

Write: Assign and provide copies of one or both writing tasks on pages 112 and 113 to students or allow them to choose. Also provide copies of the graphic organizer to help them plan their writing. Read all the directions to students to make sure they understand the task. Then have students create their ads.

Extend: If desired, have students think of things they own that they might want to sell. Have them complete the extension activity on page 113 on a separate sheet of paper.

Idea on a Hot Day

Miguel has a big lemon tree in his yard. He has an idea. He and his sister can sell lemonade on the sidewalk. Mom helps them make the lemonade. They made an ad.

Advertisement Graphic Organizer

What are you selling?

Why should people buy it?

What is the price?

Where are you selling it?

What can you draw to tell people about it?

Bake Sale Writing Task #1

Pretend that your class is having a bake sale. Your class will buy library books with the money you make. Each family will bake something. What can you bring? Make an ad for your baked goodie.

Book Sale Writing Task #2

Pretend that your library needs to make room for new books. The library is selling some old books on Saturday. All the old books will cost less than one dollar. Make an ad for the library's used-book sale.

Extension Activity

Pretend that your family is having a yard sale. You are selling some old toys. Make an ad for your toys.

Let Me Convince You

Persuasive request letters are written every day for a variety of reasons. You might want to write one to a friend requesting a special activity that you want to do. You might write a letter to a teacher or a group leader requesting that the reader choose you to be the line leader or to join the soccer team.

Once you have decided to write a request letter, you must think about the person to whom you are sending the request. You need to predict why that person might say "no" to your request. Then address those objections before you send the request. Merely repeating your viewpoint or just repeating your feelings may not convince that person. The letter should make the person you are sending it to want to read the entire explanation and realize he or she should agree with you.

A persuasive request letter should contain the following:

- a greeting
- a topic sentence with the request
- reasons using words such as *should, because,* or *that's why*
- text addressing possible concerns
- action requested of the reader
- polite wording
- a closing

The Lesson

Introduce: Using the information above, explain to students what a persuasive request letter is. Then distribute a copy of page 115 to each student. Read the scenario to students. Ask students if they have ever asked to do something and been told that they may not. Elicit the reasons.

Look at a Model: Read the model writing sample, "Jenna's Letter," to students. Talk about the reasons that Jenna gives to persuade her dad to give her permission. Discuss whether they are strong reasons. Is there anything else Jenna could have said?

Analyze the Model: Distribute a copy of the graphic organizer on page 116 to each student. Guide students through finding the information in the model writing sample to complete the graphic organizer. Some parts of the graphic organizer may not apply.

Write: Assign and provide copies of one or both writing tasks on pages 117 and 118 to students or allow them to choose. Also provide copies of the graphic organizer to help them plan their writing. Read all the directions to students to make sure they understand the task. Then have students write their persuasive request letters.

Extend: If desired, have students think of places they would like to visit. Have them complete the extension activity on page 118 on a separate sheet of paper.

Sleepover

Jenna has a new friend named Yami. Yami is having a sleepover. Jenna wants to go. But her dad doesn't want her to go. Jenna wrote a letter to her dad.

Jenna's Letter

Dear Daddy,

I really want to go to Yami's sleepover. Yami is a good friend. We will play games. Her parents are nice. But they won't let us stay up too late. You can call them. Don't worry, Daddy. Please let me go to the sleepover. I will have fun!

Love,

Jenna

Request Letter Graphic Organizer

What I want

Reason 1

Reason 2

Reason 3

Why the reader may say "no"

Why the reader should say "yes"

A Pet Writing Task #1

Pretend that you want a pet. Who do you need to ask if you can have one?
Why would he or she say "no"? Write a letter to change the person's mind.

Dear _____,

      I think we should get a _____

A Gift Writing Task #2

Pretend that there is something you want. It could be a toy, a bike, or an item of clothing. Who can you ask? Write a letter to that person.

😎 Extension Activity

Everyone in your family wants to go to a different place. Write a note to persuade your family to go to the place you chose.

Better Schools

Everyone has an opinion on how to help students do well in school. Some people propose a longer school year. Others propose building stronger support for families, such as increased access to childcare and after-school programs. Still others think that standardized testing should be reduced. Teachers, administrators, and parents all have something to say.

Young students also have opinions on how to improve their school experience. They can make a presentation to persuade adults to take action. A **presentation** is an organized way of providing information that relies heavily on graphics and minimally on text. Traditionally, it consists of a series of slides that a presenter shows as the backdrop while speaking to provide more detail. However, presentations have broadened to include infographics, display boards (often used in academic fairs), videos, and Internet presentation tools.

A persuasive presentation should contain the following:

- key statements
- details or reasons
- supporting graphics (illustrations, data)
- organization that suits the purpose
- action requested of the reader

The Lesson

Introduce: Using the information above, explain to students what a presentation is. Then distribute a copy of page 120 to each student. Read the scenario to students. Discuss what Mari's problem is. How does it affect her?

Look at a Model: Read the model writing sample, "Mari's Presentation," to students. Talk about the reasons that Mari gives to persuade the principal to change the start time. Discuss whether they are good reasons. Did Mari convince your students?

Analyze the Model: Distribute a copy of the graphic organizer on page 121 to each student. Guide students through finding the information in the model writing sample to complete the graphic organizer. Some parts of the graphic organizer may not apply.

Write: Assign and provide copies of one or both writing tasks on pages 122 and 123 to students or allow them to choose. Also provide copies of the graphic organizer to help them plan their writing. Read all the directions to students to make sure they understand the task. Then have students write their presentations.

Extend: If desired, have students make a list of what they like about school. Have them complete the extension activity on page 123 on a separate sheet of paper.

Sleepyhead

Mari has a hard time getting up in the morning. She wishes school started later. Mari has some ideas. She presented them to the principal.

Mari's Presentation

School starts at 8:15.

That is too early!

At 8:15, I'm still sleepy.

We should start at 9:00.

I am ready to learn then.

Other students feel the same way.

When should school start?

8:15

9:00

School can end later, at 3:30.

Then we can walk home with our older brother or sister.

Presentation Graphic Organizer

The problem

Details or Reasons

Picture that I will show

My solution

Why my solution is good

Name _____

Homework Writing Task #1

Some people think that homework should just be extra practice. Students should do it only if they want to. What do you think? Present your opinion and reasons.

My opinion	⇨	**My reason**

A fact	⇨	**Another fact**

My suggestion	⇨	**Why it will work**

Name _____

Recess or Art? Writing Task #2

Pretend that your school has recess in the morning and in the afternoon. The school wants to change afternoon recess to art class. What do you think? Present your opinion and reasons.

My opinion	My reason

A fact	Another fact

😎 Extension Activity

What do you like best about your school? Make a presentation to persuade other students.

We Aim to Please

When a company has a new product or service to sell, it wants to make it available as soon as possible. Sometimes the company may not be aware of what its users want or need. A service might not be accessible to people with certain disabilities. A product might not work well for all ages or ethnic backgrounds. A public place might pose problems for people with common allergies.

Sellers rely on customer feedback to know what they are doing right and, more importantly, what they are doing wrong. By understanding what the customer needs, the company can improve and grow. Business is all about pleasing the customer; responding quickly and positively to feedback usually satisfies a customer. It is also likely to bring in new customers.

Customer feedback should contain the following:
- the name of the product or service
- what you like about the product
- a description of a problem with the product
- an explanation of how the problem affects you
- a suggestion for how to fix the problem

The Lesson

Introduce: Using the information above, explain to students what feedback is. Then distribute a copy of page 125 to each student. Read the scenario to students. Discuss the purpose of an avatar. Ask students how Heba might feel.

Look at a Model: Read the model writing sample, "I Don't See Myself," to students. Discuss it, asking students to predict how the avatar company might respond to Heba's request. Help students understand the customer–business relationship and how each side needs the other.

Analyze the Model: Distribute a copy of the graphic organizer on page 126 to each student. Guide students through finding the information in the model writing sample to complete the graphic organizer. Some parts of the graphic organizer may not apply.

Write: Assign and provide copies of one or both writing tasks on pages 127 and 128 to students or allow them to choose. Also provide copies of the graphic organizer to help them plan their writing. Read all the directions to students to make sure they understand the task. Then have students write their feedback.

Extend: If desired, have students brainstorm other changes they would like to have made. Help them identify who could make the change and who needs their feedback. Have them complete the extension activity on page 128 on a separate sheet of paper.